Socialmedia Influence
Currency of the Future

By
Michael Light

Michael Light

Contents

Michael Light

Dedication

I hope that some people completely disagree with every idea in this book! I would like to thank you personally for the motivation to write your dissent. I expect that some people will resonate with the entire concept, but like a good moral, it isn't for the wise that we jest!

I have spent my whole life surrounded by good advice like; "get a job with good benefits and save money!" I'm just glad I never listened. I think that this advice paves the way to a collective narcotic addiction to behavior.

I would however like to thank the entire World for being a part of this masterpiece called Life. I love that, as a whole, we are unpredictable and leaderless in the face of total uncertainty. Without you and the beautiful qualities that make you truly unique, the entire Internet would have never been worth paying attention to.

I would also like to thank the students that walked out of the LA School District and Rupert Murdoch for being yourself. Without you guys I might have missed the entire theme of this book!

And, thank you God for evolution! It sure seems to constantly surprise the fuck out of me! ...what a crazy game you're rolling!

Introduction

Influence is everywhere. It's smeared all over nature. It takes many different forms and forms many different things. Something as easy and natural as an agreement between people can set a proxy that is mutable and effectual. In other words, our choices can be shared. If we come together around an idea and decide how we are going to apply some value to it, we call it a dollar. First it was silver and gold, and then there were Greenbacks. Before that it was shells and beads, and before that... survival!

Since the dawn of time, humanity's quest for influence has always come through the medium of communication. Throughout our entire history we have been hard at work, developing more and more sophisticated forms of technology to enhance this endeavor, to connect our influence with others. It is a natural phenomena of humanity to seek out and formulate lasting communities, and as long as everything is good... It's All Good!

The epic tools for this task are to see and hear what we're communicating with each other. To directly feel the presence of our community. When I am communicating directly with another person, I know that with a bit of luck, we are going to figure things out, and together we've developed influence. First with each other, and then together as one greater influence than the sum of it's parts, so to speak.

Writing this book was an inquiry, for me, into the idea of influence and socialmedia. It started four years ago when MySpace shut down their chat feature for "repairs." It stayed offline for weeks. At the time, MySpace was a living system of people sharing influence and forming communities. Turning off that feature was like a ten-million-way train wreck! If you were to measure the currency, impacted by that, that's what you would see shift.

Encompassing the millions of people chatting are WORLDS of real events that are being directly affected *and* effected by that communication. This is real influence. Ironically, two million LA County students used the MySpace chat feature to organize a walkout that day! They did it to protest an unpopular emigration law. And I will never see the World the same way again.

Michael Light

Chapter 1 - The Birth of Cool... Not!

This evolution of communication has brought us to a place we now refer to as "Online Socialmedia". Socialmedia sites like Facebook, Twitter and Klout are changing almost everything about our lives right now. Some of these changes are obvious, while others are slightly less noticeable. Some may never be noticed, or even understood, for years. So, where did this thing come from and why is it so popular?

Well, if we were to mark the beginning of this amazing phenomena, it would probably be the Bulletin Boards of the late 1970's. Some of the early nerds may remember the bulletin board.

These earlier forms of socialmedia were similar to the group pages on Facebook. The main difference being that one could browse and share files, as well as read the daily status updates. These boards were originally hosted on those dinosaur IBM "Big Blue" computers that were located on university campuses or in government buildings. The original purpose was to speed the process of sharing data over long distances, or with several participating parties.

Later on, when smaller personal computers came of age, a bulletin board could be hosted privately and was generally moderated by the computer's owner. Anyone who wanted access to it had to get permission from the host. You would receive a username and password in order to gain deeper access than you could reach as a guest. It allowed guests to see what was being posted on the main board, but protected the files below, that were often

not rated PG. Hackers would share things about sites and software on these hidden harddrives as well.

In those days, an archaic modem was needed to plug in your telephone line, in order to connect with these mainframe servers. These old modems looked like something out of the Flintstones. It had two gray rubber cups and you literally plugged your phone receiver into it, which allowed you to "dial-up" the computer hosting the server. Once this was done, the two computers would start beeping and chirping bytes back and forth to establish a connection between each other. (I hate that I know this stuff...)

Bulletin boards may have been a shade off gray when it came to the Internet's current look and feel, but the main ideas were there. It was a place to form a community with other nerds who had similar interests. I don't think any of them were anything like famous, but I'm sure that tons of old programs and maybe even some hardware projects were corroborated using them. Oh... and I almost forgot, it was as slow as it ever was!

Michael Light

Chapter 2 - Realtime

In the early 60's, a system was being developed which allowed the Big Blue computers to communicate with each other around the World in real time. This system, which would eventually be called the Internet, used clear glass cables (fiber optics) and converted the data into light, reversing the process on the other end. It was connected though a network of servers which caught the packets of data and then shot it to the next server, until it reached it's final destination. This system increased not only the speed, but also the amount of data, or bandwidth, that could be transfered from place to place. It was the original gateway to realtime interactive conferencing, which is the basic idea behind the cumulative socialmedia sphere. It was soon opened up to anyone with a computer and a modem. There was only one small problem. Nerds built it!

So, even though the Internet initially gave us access to the World Wide Web of information, it was still pretty limited to computer geeks. In order to navigate your way around it, you had to know a bit of code. You'd have to be able to "load" programs and "run" them. Plus everything was in HTML code, which looks a bit like Chinese written in Greek. But, that soon changed!

It was an amazing shift when the graphical user interface (GUI) showed up. We were finally able to surf the World's information base virtually, using a mouse and simply clicking buttons. This made the new World Wide Web environment "user friendly!" It finally introduced cyberspace as the new frontier of communication. After this anyone with a computer could understand how to use it, and we really began to see the potential that had seemed so illusive... and then it came to life in 256 colors. (Ooh!) Suddenly it was a World of pictures and places we had only seen before in magazines. It was now a global community of real people with personal experiences that we could form a relationships around. It included email and search engines and tons of information that would grow more and more fascinating by the day.

Michael Light

Chapter 3 - Size Means Everything

Since the beginning of the personal computer revolution, we have seen **everything** in our lives begin to change into some kind of crazy, surrealistic science fiction. It has exploded exponentially with each new advance in device technology. Processor speed, hardware, software, bandwidth and imagination, as well as access, have come together to give us a platform with which we can share more and more information with more and more frequency. Today I can respond to an email, check my Facebook status updates with my iPhone and watch "tweets" originating from the New York Stock Market Floor, all while riding the lightrail to work, in almost any city around the Globe. Ladies and Gentlemen, buckle your seatbelts... The future is here!

In the year 2000, now dubbed "Y2K", there were 124 million Americans connected to the Internet. Most of them on a dial-up connection. By this time, fortunately, you could just plug the phone line directly into your computer. By 2010 that number more than doubled to 311 million connections, practically all of them highspeed. Today there are more wifi hot spots than anyone can count; in coffeehouses, restaurants, hotels, airports, and commuter trains, all over the World. Even airlines have jumped on the bandwagon and offer wifi services on many overland flights. It's definitely gone viral! And, with so much free and pay use access, and not just wifi, but also smart phones and smart pads, the entire Earth's stream of growing information has shrunk to the size of a small device you can hold in your hand. This has advanced the momentum of a renaissance in global communication. Who would have guessed that that first calculator chip (Intel 4004: first processor) held the key to such a major shift in our global perception?

During this new era, socialmedia became more and more popular. Companies began racing to be the centerpiece of the rapidly growing and developing socialmedia culture. A first major player to break ranks was Yahoo. The next major player award would have to go to MySpace, which peaked in members sometime around 2007, and has been in a steady decline ever since it took sides over a LA County School District walkout. Next came the new and current reigning champion; Facebook!

Now, in 2011, the average adult is spending more and more time on Facebook. Their website has managed to eclipse every other socialmedia site on the Internet with a staggering 750 million members, from all over the globe. They are currently adding around 10 million new members a month. Facebook has successfully become the epicenter of an entire cultural shift that logs on daily to check their friends' status updates, respond to being tagged in their friends' pictures, and chat with whomever of their friends happen to be online... A LOT!

Michael Light

Chapter 4 - The New Pioneers of Socialmedia

Now you have to keep in mind that in the early days of computing, the entire generation was spoon fed a lifestyle of suits and ties. Math was done with a slide rule, and the **men of** IBM and the model they were presenting to the World was all we knew about computers. A computer was a business tool and NOT a toy! Steve Jobs saw the World quite differently. He saw the computer as a revolution.

I sometimes wonder if he saw the World that I look around and see right now, in a vision – maybe he had a glimpse of the future. While everyone else seemed happy enough just to be able to get access to a computer (I'm obviously talking about the nerds here), he somehow saw an entire social shift.

He has been at every corner of just about every new technology that has taken us forward by leaps! The iPhone, for instance, gives anyone in the World the ability to be the eyes and ears of the whole global community, at any given moment. This is not your IBM suit and tie perspective at all!

After successfully moving Apple out of Steve Wozniak's garage and positioned as a competitive company, Jobs got a call from an office down the road that housed a small Research & Development department of Xerox. Xerox felt they were a copier company and not a computer company. The Xerox research department at PARC, in Palo Alto, had a few inventions under their belt, and the engineers decided to give them to Apple. These inventions were the mouse and the Graphical User Interface. Ironically, Steve Jobs hired Microsoft to write the software to run these new inventions, which they did, but did it for their new operating system... Windows! Jobs, on the other hand, believing the future to be about amazing over accomplishments, started a project called Lisa with the new technology. The Lisa turned out to be too expensive for the market, but it showed everyone the integrity of Steve Jobs' sometimes crazy desire for innovation. After all, he was leading a revolution! Remember the first Macintosh commercial? In the commercial, a girl runs into a room filled with people watching a Big Brother scene and throws a big sludge hammer at it. It was directed by Ridley Scott and titled "1984".

Before the Internet, the early PC's and Mac's were pretty much nerd-only devices, as I've mentioned. Anyone who used it had to know a bit of tech code in order to access and run programs. This was hardly a mainstream fad. There were tons of programs being written, but the early front runners were business programs like, Wordstar and dBase. This was all part of the old IBM dominance, and it would shape a lot of the early market. On the other side of this equation was the artistic side of the market that were following the Mac's, which were loaded with more random access memory and could facilitate the need for faster graphics. In the background were the socialmedia junkies and hackers, who mostly traded in pirated software and pornographic file sharing through the early bulletin boards. The most famous hacker was Kevin Mitnick, who, after being arrested, became one of the best computer security consultants out there. These guys were originally called tweekers, but now that has entirely different connotations.

With the introductions of Windows and the Macintosh, we began to glimpse the revolution of an Internet with unlimited potential, darkly at first, as Paul says, but it finally became "user friendly." Bulletin Boards were replaced with file sharing and email, while other forms of socialmedia began to develop, inviting people to sign up for free! Some of the early attempts into this new World are still around. Sites like Hotmail – now MSN Hotmail – and Yahoo, which could be accessed through the now extinct browser Netscape Navigator. These were some of the originators of the socialmedia direction online. Finally the days of the green screen were replaced with the soft blue glow and socialmedia was starting come into focus.

Originally known as "David and Jerry's guide to the World Wide Web," Yahoo began in 1995 as a searchable data base. In 2007 they added email, blogging, and groups, which allowed members to exchange ideas and post opinions about any topic under the sun. Ironically, most of the interaction on the early attempts at socialmedia got whittled down to less exchanging of ideas and much more bantering, but the model of socialmedia sites were beginning to explode, some using the success of sites like Yahoo to model their look and feel. Dubbed the "Information Superhighway," the Internet had finally become popular in the mainstream. Within no time at all, almost everyone I know had a Yahoo email address or a blog and began spending more and more time online. And finally, the monkeys were able to fling poo at will!

Then came the advantageous and annoying banner ads and click-through advertising. It soon became as common as milk in the fridge. Pop-ups and lots of "in your face" reminders of the old media dinosaurs filled the small spaces and gaps in between everything. As the internet's first business model, tons companies were racing onto the scene, hurrying to get on board. This was the heyday of the dotcom bubble. Everyone was making hand over foot money, selling more crap in a World they hardly understood. Having no idea that they were building their own pitfall, people began jumping into every new startup without even looking, and on the horizon the clouds were beginning to darken.

Michael Light

Chapter 5 - The Dotcom Bomb - 2000

Within a few years of what Alan Greenspan coined "irrational exuberance" over the millions of new web start-ups, the explosion of web frenzy collapsed into the "Dot Com Bomb." I like to think of it as the big filter, because it weeded out a ton of bad habits that had formed around the ease with which people could take advantage of each other, often preying on each others' excitement about this growing market. On the other hand, this catastrophic event decimated a ton of free services, like free online phone services, free web hosting and email services, and sent giant ripples through the entire economy.

Companies like Netscape completely disappeared from the scene while others managed to survive.

Many of the survivors became some of the core companies of the modern Internet environment. Most of these companies survived the big filter because they had excellent financial plans that were built around the psychology of the user, rather than the providers or advertisers. Some companies like Google were doing this, spending a lot of energy on algorithms that made their services more efficient as well as creating innovative financial models others would follow down the road.

In late 1999, my girlfriend and I traveled to Portland just before the whole mess exploded. Our goal was to move there and play music. This was an amazing time. Technology that had previously been too expensive for me to invest in was now becoming affordable for anyone. We were able to get all of our music equipment and a desktop computer for less than 2K. I immediately went to work in our spare bedroom and we recorded all of our music in a little over a month.

After that we were able to use dialpad.com, a free

online phone, to set up gigs. We created a press package with graphics software we bought. I built a website, promoted our online presence, and we played gigs all over Portland for the next year. This was an exciting time for us. It was my first glimpse into a future that was about creative and social self-empowerment. We had access to tools that were once reserved for people with deep pockets, and now things like a recording studio and distribution were practically free. Unfortunately, a lot of the things that were making it all possible crashed during the big filter, but man was that a great time!

At the time, one thing seemed certain to me; these were the tools I had been waiting my whole life for, and the Internet was the way to creative freedom. The combination of software and access to things that were unthinkable a few years before, were now very real and would probably come back once the dust settled. With nothing more than a computer and an Internet connection, anyone with talent could now create and promote their own work with socialmedia. I could connect to everywhere, and would never need an agent or a curator to decide my fate again.

When I was a kid I got a small preview of what was to come when my mom's boyfriend would take me to work with him. He was a programmer on an old Big Blue IBM. He sat me down at a console one day and showed me the basics. Then I spent the next few months hacking the entire system. Every time he'd bring me along I would wonder the halls of virtual directories and search for games to play in all the areas of the network I could find. I had access to an entire World Wide Web of opportunity, and had no idea that it was just the beginning!

Michael Light

Chapter 6 - The Murdoch Rule...

Don't cut yourself shaving!

In early 2008, at the peak of the MySpace phenomena, something incredible happened that would change my perception of socialmedia forever. This was around the same time that Tila Tequila had reached a stellar 100 thousand friends on MySpace and turned her socialmedia presence into a catapult for a very lucrative professional career. Her popularity there landed her tons of modeling work, and eventually scored her a show on MTV. I would even be willing to dub her the World's first socialmedia super star. Although, in and of itself, that is an amazing use of socialmedia, that's not the event that blew my mind. What did it for me was the LA School District student walkout on March 30, 2008. Almost every student in Los

Angeles schools walked out of classes to protest an unpopular immigration law that was going to threaten the autonomy of the entire Los Angeles Latino Community. The walkout, and the protest that was held at the civic center, was planned and executed using the MySpace chat feature, and then something unusual happened... enter Rupert Murdoch.

Some of you may know Rupert Murdoch, who, as a major national media mogul and owner of Fox News, had acquired MySpace in 2005. Now, I'm not really sure if he was asked to do this, but during the student walkouts in LA, either he or MySpace swiftly shut down the chat feature. After it was reported that the MySpace chat feature was used to organize the student walkout, the MySpace chat feature vanished! On their website, MySpace said that the feature was having some problems which were being resolved. It ended up being offline for something like 6 weeks. And, when it finally reappeared, guess what? ... You had to "sign-up" for it. I was disgusted, and not just because I hate signing up for crap when people already have my information, but because I felt like this was how Rupert Murdoch's old dinosaur media thinking was going to try and take over our autonomy, or spy on us. Well, that was it for me! I decided to look into Facebook as an alternative, even though I thought it was a little bland and not very intuitive. At least it had a chat feature that just worked and I didn't have to sign up for it again.

I saw this event as the first brush stroke of the renaissance. People were actually using socialmedia for real change, and it was a threat to the current paradigm. It really showed me that human beings were sympathetic toward their own community and when they worked together they could make a difference using socialmedia. I grew up in the peak of the cold war and felt constantly haunted by the threat of nuclear war. It made me, and an entire generation, feel totally powerless, but this was different. It wasn't a mass rally to protest an unconscious war. It was to honor a part of our own community, and Rupert Murdoch's reaction to it really surprised me. I probably shouldn't have been surprised at all, actually. Looking back I should have expected it. The old guard probably saw this as a pretty major threat to their ideology of "keeping the masses quelled" in order to avoid the fears of Freud, while the real problem is not the unruly mob, but rather the false assessment of humanity inherent in that notion. I believe that there is a natural survival mechanism that dates back to tribal existence. The tribe itself is far more likely to survive if the whole works for the good of the tribe.

Michael Light

Chapter 7 - Human Ingredients

Recent studies by Technology Lab at Stanford University came to the conclusion that online users seem to exhibit certain common characteristics that are consistent. These include, but are not limited to (in my opinion); competence, autonomy and relatedness, and according to their research, when these three ingredients are present in the right measure it can lead someone to, "take action," like following a link to read a blog or "get a free" whatever. I would be willing to chance a guess that the opposite is true as well; not taking action, or taking a negative action, like leaving MySpace for Facebook.

They also believe that people have already existing motivations (shocking but true) that cause users to follow links related to their own motivations, which seems kind of obvious when you think about it. The goal itself, since it's a business research team, is to somehow place "hot triggers" in the path of these existing or inspired "motivations," which will lead to people "taking action." I do agree with the basic psychology in this study, but I don't think it's new. I do however see human intelligence catching on, when it comes to the old media dinosaur tricks. Personally I think the whole study is a bit too "IBM in a gray suit" for me. It really seems to disregard the natural sympathetic nature of human beings, which is an innate characteristic of the human survival mechanism. Our desire to help others and relate is as natural as waking up in the morning, and for some it is easier than others, but we all do it.

Psychology in media, as I mentioned previously, is nothing new. It was born in the early 1900's, around the end of the first World War. If it had a father, that father would be a man named Edward Bernays. Edward Bernays, nephew of Sigmund Freud, was asked to accompany Woodrow Wilson to the signing of the Versailles treaty, at the end of the first World War. His task was to use his talents in a new form of propaganda that he called "Public Relations." He was issued the task to sell Woodrow Wilson's "League of Nations" idea to the World's most powerful nations. This, according to Wilson, would ensure World peace and avoid any future public resentments that might someday "rise up" and threaten Democracy.

This angle of perception has always been at the root of public relations, according to Edward Bernays. His uncle Sigmund believed that destructive forces were inherent in humanity, and that under the right circumstances these forces could be unleashed in the form of the "unruly mob" if they were not somehow controlled.

Edward Bernays' style of psychology-driven Public Relations set many precedents for the PR and Advertising industries for years to come, in print media, radio and television. Ironically, Bernays' style of PR work fits directly into Stanford's research ideas about online users. Phrases like, "4 out of 5 Doctors Recommend," give people sound reasoning to make their own decisions more wisely. This reflects directly on the natural desire for people to feel competent, autonomous, and related. At least it did in the 50's.

I love the line in the second Matrix movie, when Neo is listening to the Architect, who says, "99% of all test subjects accepted the programming as long as they were given a choice, even if they were only aware of that choice at a near subconscious level". The problem is choice, and Edward Bernays, using insights he had gained from reading his uncle's first book on psychoanalysis, learned how to address the problem using psychology. The grave misconception behind this model of advertising and PR, is that it considers humanity to be "unruly" at it's core, which requires some form of outside control in order to prevent the angry "mob" from unleashing. Ironically, no one had ever even heard of Freud until Edward Bernays made him famous.

Although Freud's theories could have a lot to do with this brilliant and suppressive use of psychoanalytical non-sense in order to maintain peace among human beings, it is likely that the real fuel behind the PR industry was actually the manufacturing industry. During WWI hundreds of factories were built to support the war efforts in Europe. After the war, a lot of these factories were faced with shutting down unless they could keep the wheels of growth moving, and the best way to do this was to get people to want to buy things they really didn't need. They needed a consumer base in order to survive, and turned to Edward Bernays to create one for them.

This fit perfectly into the desire of those poisoned by Freud into thinking that humanity was a threat to democratic leadership. It gave the powerful a way to distract the masses into voluntary submission as consumers living the American Dream! Television became the camp fire we gathered around in our modern society, which offered the next few generations a slew of hot-triggers and motivation, which we labeled alternatively... "keeping up with the Jones'"! All brought to you by major branding and celebrity endorsements, for a safe and secure society!

With the Internet, the problem of choice is being revisited again, and the lesson of Rupert Murdoch may very well have been the first shot fired in a revolution. The old media-driven-PR control model must have thought that shutting down the chat feature would be just like canceling a commercial or a show that gave the wrong message or empowerment. Unfortunately for Rupert Murdoch, this choice only succeeded in destroying MySpace's credibility with the socialmedia fan base. It was just like giving away his hard-earned market shares to whoever wanted to be next! This also tells us something that is not in the Stanford Research notes... That the Internet is like a multi-headed hydra, and if you cut off a head on this amorphous leaderless family of chatters and socialites, one will grow back that makes the first look like a molehill to Mt Everest. The irony is that some of the old meida moguls still don't get it!

Michael Light

Chapter 8 - The Facebook Nebula

In 2003, a Harvard student named Mark
Zuckerberg developed a website similar to "Hot or
Not." Leave it to a hacker to create a site using
images he stole (hacked) from the Harvard student
database. The site was originally called Facemash
and got shut down within a month. It wouldn't be
the last time Zuckerberg would be investigated for
questionable tactics.

Originally dubbed "TheFaceBook," Zuckerberg and
his cohorts successfully built a social site that was,
at the time, limited to Harvard students only. It
would later be opened up to other Ivy league
colleges and eventually all colleges as well as high
school students. Now anyone 13+ can sign up for an
account.

In late 2011, Facebook had grown to an astounding 750 million members from all around the World. At the time of this writing it stands poised to overtake Google as the most visited website on the Internet. Studies vary, but say that the average adult spends between 15-45 minutes on Facebook every time they go online. It often starts with a message; "Dave tagged you in one of his photos"! So, you hop over and check to be sure it's not embarrassing and the next thing you know, you've spent 15 minutes there, and then 10 more updating and checking the daily feed, before finally realizing that you're supposed to be working...

There are several reasons why Facebook has become such a successful site. The first is their financial model. It gave them a really strong foundation to build on. Some people consider the Facebook method of AdSence a bit invasive, when it comes to how they use our personal information, but all in all this format of advertising is pretty inert and can easily be ignored. Although businesses have requested that Facebook open up their advertising for more trademarking to be direct to more users, at an recent influence summit, my hope is we don't get dinosaur TV promotion style ads in the future.

The most obvious aspect of Facebook's success is their user model. Facebook has successfully brought together many of the previously fragmented parts of socialmedia. Yahoo attempted this in the early days, but due to the front end search model, it failed to bring everything together the way Facebook does through their personal pages. People can not only post their thoughts in their daily status, but can also post pictures, videos and notes. We can instant message or even send messages like email to each other. We can even create our own special pages for a business or our favorite pet. It's pretty complete when you consider all the options.

The other thing that makes Facebook a safe environment to put up our personal pages is the autonomy we each have as users. This is something MySpace didn't do and I think it kept some people at bay. Not everyone wants the whole World to see everything they have to post. Some people keep their friends list to just that, while others love to accept every invitation they get, but the choice is our own.

Facebook has also created an entirely new way of seeing the Internet as more of a community than a commercial or retail platform, while not excluding it, by allowing apps to integrate directly into it. Anyone can build a game, a website, or a socialmedia platform and connect it to Facebook via an app. Apps, or applications, have become an everyday feature for the mainstream user on everything from computers to handheld devices. If someone wants to look up a good place to eat, they generally reach into their pocket and click on an app to find out what is nearby, or read the reviews of places they are visiting for the first time. Apps can also be use for field reporting or event tracking. One of my friends recently used her iPhone to update her Facebook page while she ran her first marathon. It was great for us, the crowd at home, who could see how she was doing the whole time.

By the time the race was over there were a dozen people cheering her on! It was like being there.

Different applications can also plug into Facebook and share statuses or report when a new blog is written in Wordpress. This is a very different paradigm. It gives other sites access through the Facebook API, and also invites people to leave the Facebook site, which was considered an early taboo. Most people were trying everything they could, early on, to keep their guest "theirs," and here's Facebook literally giving away their members and the information links to their members. How Absurd! This paradigm was the best change that has ever happened in the history of the socialmedia realm, if you ask me! It gave everyone the message that we are a community. Brilliant! Facebook has literally become the socialmedia hub of the vast nebula it is connected to and unless they go pull a Murdoch, they will continue to be a huge part of the future of socialmedia.

Michael Light

Chapter 9 - The Twitter Effect!

Twitter, originally "twttr" was conceived in a meeting at Odeo, later purchased by the founders of Twitter, and was based on the theme of an online SMS service. Jack Dorsey sent the first Tweet on March 21st 2006 at 9:50 PM. Twitter has been at the epicenter of several World events when regular communications shut down.

When I tell my new clients I'll be signing them up on Twitter, the first thing they do is roll their eyes and give me some excuse for why they think that isn't necessary. I think most people may feel that way for a few different reasons. One of the main reasons is than when you first look at Twitter it seems a bit pointless if all you can do is type a status, and on top of that it is limited to 140 symbols total, and what can anyone need that for?

The other reason I think it's taken longer for people to catch on to it, is that it came in to popularity right behind the MySpace/Facebook transition. Most people didn't start into socialmedia until Facebook caught on, at least not the mainstream portion. MySpace was a bit too fruity and event driven to really take hold with most mainstream users, who really only used the Internet for email. Now practically everyone's Mom and Grandma has a Facebook account. Some friends of mine were afraid their parents were going to friend them, and it really scared them away from posting certain things, but that's all changing. Now they are faced with a new socialmedia software that doesn't really make enough sense to justify even trying Twitter out.

Twitter is definitely the most brilliant advance in socialmedia since the chat feature. Some of the things that Twitter can do, many other socialmedia sites like Foursquare or Facebook probably never will. Let's start with the Haiti Earthquake.

According to Jeremy Rifkin, immediately following the Haiti earthquake, Twitters began tweeting within the first 2 minutes, followed by YouTube footage, and within a short period of time the entire World knew about it. Millions of dollars were sent in the form of assistance to help and, with that, the first ripples of the Twitter Effect were felt.

Another event, which went almost entirely overlooked by the US media, was the situation on the ground in Bahrain. It followed the Egyptian democratic movement and due to American Politics was ignored by the media. Not unlike Egypt, peaceful demonstrations were held in the capital. The difference being that this one was suppressed by the Saudi Military, which was sent in to end the demonstrations. In Libya, America has sent in tons of assistance to the victims of the same type of actions. I tried to follow it through alternative media sources, but found little to no reporting being done. I finally checked Twitter to see if I could get some news on what was happening, starting with a regional search. With Twitter I am able to pick a region, which allows me to see all the

Tweets coming from just that place. Once I had figured out some of the hash-tags being associated with the Tweets. I was able to literally watch what was happening in real-time, on the ground. In turn, I became one of the few American writers that were posting events as they occurred, linking them from my blog to my Facebook account.

There are a couple of thoughts that come to mind when I consider the viral nature of these different events. On one hand, considering the Haiti earthquake, people were able to respond in a way that fit the basic outcome of the Stanford research mentioned earlier. They could pick up their cell phone, hand-held, or sit down at their computer and respond by sending money to help the victims there. They were motivated by what they saw on YouTube and were able to autonomously take action, which gave them a feeling of doing something that helped others. On the other hand, the situation in Bahrain was a bit different. Even though a lot of people were spreading news about the event, there was really no way for anyone to act. It essentially left people with a feeling of helplessness just to read into it. You couldn't just push a link that led you to a way that could help anyone. One of the actions people might have taken could have been boycotting oil, but that kind of action can't be seen as a benefit to people who count on their vehicle to support their own lives and families. It was probably never even considered by most of the people who took notice, and sacrificing our own lifestyle in order to help others may still be some time off, at least in this country. In time though, we may see Twitter at the heart of much more communication as we see many changes happening in the World, especially if they affect us directly or play into our ability to act.

Some of Twitter's other functions are the ability to @mention people or follow #hash marked trending phrases or words that are hot topic in the news, or even "follow" things or people that are popular on television. We can also choose to follow anyone we want who has a Twitter account, without having to get an okay from them in order to see their posts. We can even look through the list of other people they follow and follow them as well.

I use it to link everything else to one action. I can post links to things I think are important without having to reword or rewrite the content, which not only gets the message out, but also supports the writers of good content worth sharing. I can notify my entire network when I post a new blog. I can even use it to keep in contact with someone across the Globe with its message feature, and like Facebook, Twitter lets other apps connect to it by giving those apps permissions to post my tweets as well as post to my Twitter account. Twitter now has 200 million members, who Tweet over 150 million tweets a day. I have the app on my iPhone and use it for several different reasons, but sometimes I use it to tweet a thought!

Michael Light

Chapter 10 - YouTube Gone Viral

YouTube is, as most everyone knows, a place where you can post and view videos. It has been responsible for helping the World to see things happening in various places. It has taught us, through tutorials, everything from yoga to using specific softwares. If I ever need a howto, the first place I check is YouTube, because seeing is believing.

YouTube is also a way for events to reach the general public; as I mentioned, most of the World found out about the tragedy in Haiti through YouTube. This has had a secondary effect, which is forcing Governments and the media to be more honest. We don't need the mainstream media any longer to find out what is happening around the World. In fact, I seem to be getting most of my news flashes now from Facebook, which I often follow up on with YouTube to get more of the story. It's not just funny cat videos.

YouTube is a very important socialmedia platform that allows us to film events and report to the World what we see. This makes everyone on the planet a potential field agent. A hands on reporter that can often report directly, without the media slant we get with most news agencies. I don't mind reading the paper, but please stop telling me why something is happening. This is an old dinosaur media trick that paints the World with news instead of reporting it. YouTube can cut right through the BS with unedited media, leaving us free to draw our own conclusions. Back, and to the left!

I am curious to see how YouTube will reinvent itself though. This morning I saw an article that said more people were watching videos on Facebook,

which I think is pretty cool, while I would like to see more sites doing socialmedia rather than less! I think it is important to have many facets to the diamond. It makes it stronger and less susceptible to any kind of authoritative push. Even though I know that nothing can stop something no one controls!

One of the things everyone seems to be pursuing in the World of socialmedia is the viral effect that takes a message to millions of hits. I have read everything I could find about why people think they know or understand why it happens – why it is that some videos become so popular that everyone is sharing it with someone else. If you take into consideration all the different types of videos that go viral, it is easy to see there is no specific golden rule. Some people say that the secret ingredient is content. Others believe it is humor, and some believe it to be promotion of how and where we place our links to the existing videos we produce, but frankly I think it is beyond any specific detail that makes a video viral out into the World.

One of the videos mentioned in "Barack Inc." is a video called "Evolution." It was produced by Dove soap and looks at the process of creating a makeup billboard from start to finish in time-lapsed photography. It starts with a pretty typical girl who is taken through the paces of becoming a beautiful creation through makeup, photography and Photoshop. They even enlarge her eyes! It's pretty crazy. The ad ends with a short statement about our perception of beauty and links to a site the helps people with self-esteem issues. It's pretty brilliant, in my opinion, and has managed to score an incredible 15 million hits.

Most of the top scores in the Viral League are music videos (not surprising) with Justin Bieber holding the number one spot with half a billion hits. In fact the top ten videos on YouTube are all music videos except one called "Charley bit me," which is a couple kids being filmed and one keeps putting his finger in the others mouth, and guess what?! The other kid bites him... WTF? This video is responsible for a whopping 375 million hits. I think it's a pretty unlikely candidate for a viral video, and this one ranks about 5th of all time on YouTube. These examples completely alleviate the intelligence that the Dove video presents, and "Charley" in particular completely baffles me.

Viral video, to me, seems a lot like the movie industry when it comes to what's hot. Even the actors working on the movie Star Wars had no idea it was going to be such an amazing success, just as J.K. Rowling probably had no idea her books would be such a success. The trick seems to be uniquely creative and probably innocent inspiration, that is the real power behind videos that reach the status of viral. One thing is for sure though; YouTube's ability to propel a video to viral is a huge tool in the quest for influence. It may even play a huge part in the evolution of global society.

Michael Light

Chapter 11 - The Standard for Influence

I hate to admit this, but one day I was watching a Socialmedia panel discussion on YouTube. At one point the discussion members started asking each other what their Klout scores were. It was completely new for me to hear people ask each other this question, so I Googled it and found a video of an interview with Joe Fernandez. In this interview he was discussing a new K+ feature that Klout was introducing. Well, it turns out that Klout is a website that measures your online socialmedia influence. It uses several different metrics to come up with an overall score between 1 and 100. You sign into it using either Twitter or Facebook and it looks at all your interactions online to produce your socialmedia influence score.

The metrics Klout looks at are things like "total network," "amplification probability," and "true reach." It even looks into loopholes like bots (fake profile robots). The algorithms are designed by 16 Phd's according to Joe Fernandez, and they are always looking to fine tune the entire process in order to keep it as accurate as possible. And just because you may not know anything about it, don't think for one moment that you aren't being scored even as we speak. The fact is that many companies are taking advantage of the Klout API and may have already checked your score, if you have checked into a hotel, flown recently, or even rented a car. According to Joe, some companies are even offering perks to their customers if there score is high enough. Other companies have sent their products to members of Klout with a specific score range to test and write about their products. Klout has made it clear to these companies however, that their members will always have the right to write whatever they want about the products they receive. This week a major magazine announced that Klout was one of the 50 best websites on the web.

One of the challenges for Klout, looking forward, is going to be similar to the challenges that search engines had with clever people. One of the videos I saw that dubbed itself a Klout tutorial, was done by this guy who showed how to pick the people you followed based on a Google Chrome plug-in that shows everyones Klout score right on your Twitter feed. Personally I would keep stuff like that to myself if I engaged in those kinds of tactics, but this guy was teaching people how to do it. Google actually boots people from their search results when they are found using less than genuine strategies to increase their search position. It seems likely that until Klout can get the bugs out of their algorithms and learn to keep those discoveries secret, they are going to be constantly challenged by people who still don't get what socialmedia is really about. Regardless of whether or not Klout is the Standard, the idea of socialmedia as a *currency* is hugely profound.

In the real World, I use Klout as a meter for my clients to be able to gauge my progress on their socialmedia network. Once I have everything set up and connected I sign them up for Klout and send them the link so they can see their own score. It allows them to see for themselves that what I am doing is working. It's nice for me too, because most of the people I work with on socialmedia presence don't really understand it at first. With Klout, they can see a number that tells them something they can relate to. Some people seem to use it to get perks, while others seem to think that if they have a high Klout score they will get more work when people see how good they are at socialmedia. I think that's great, but I spend so much time on my client work that I sometimes horribly neglect my own socialmedia presence... sometimes for weeks, which causes my score to bounce way up and down a lot. It kind of reminds me of what the stock market looks like right now. Especially now that I'm working on this book! lol :P

I wonder if Klout will include other arrays in the measure of influence and include major events. I would be deeply interested in seeing how these things look in numbers, like an earthquake, or a revolution. It could tell us about the significance of certain news pieces or primary elections. One of the things that keeps people separate is not knowing how others feel about things. It would be amazing to track how people felt about breast cancer or autism, and how those feelings were being effected by campaigns that are set-up to bring more awareness, or to help fund treatments. I definitely like what Klout is doing and really want to see more. It would be amazing to see real values on anything we can imagine. Have it on a platform like Google, where we can search it out to see how it ranks on the global influence scene.

Klout has amplified the idea of socialmedia influence as a currency. The way I generally explain this to people is simple. Most of us can agree that we probably wouldn't even bother to show up to work if we weren't getting paid for it. If we look at money in this way, it has the power to influence people to do things they probably wouldn't do otherwise. There are levels of this idea around us in every walk of life. Here's another consideration. If you ask anyone the question, "what is the most influential thing on Earth?", many people will agree it is the US Dollar. Look at all the turmoil it's caused recently with the US debt crisis. It has been shaking up much more than just the economy. It has been shaking up everyone's loyalty to it, while socialmedia influence has been gaining strength. Coincidence?

Michael Light

Chapter 12 - A Brief History of Currency Influence

No one really knows for sure when currency came into being, but if we consider the art of the cuneiform, it looks like a trade between a corn farmer and an ox herder. The art is a picture of a man holding three ears of corn and below it is an ox. My thinking is that it was compressing the form of the corn farmers yield so that he could get an ox right away to till his field. Instead of trusting the farmer to do good on his word, he asked him to etch it in stone. This is likely to be one of the first forms of compressing time and space.

Regardless to the accuracy of my thoughts about cuneiforms, it would seem to me that whatever form of currency we use in trade represents a compressed form of time, space, information, process, or technology. It frees an individual or group from the need to carry around a goat on their shoulders in order to buy a loaf of bread. It's pretty common knowledge that an endless stream of ideas have fit the currency bill, from shells to beads and gold to paper. We've literally tried everything under the sun, including direct trade which covers everything else. Currency itself, ultimately, is a tool.

About 12k-14k years ago, according to Dr. Jared Diamond, through archaeological finds along the Dead Sea, surpluses of grains gave rise to specialization skills like metallurgy and early chemistry. The archaeological finds were something like raised floors, which Dr. Diamond considers to have been the first granaries. This ability to store grains allowed one to accumulate much more than an individual may have needed for one season. The resulting surplus could have freed up members of the tribe to discover other skills. This would have been a source key for specialization. It led to many technological advances, like CPA's and nuclear physicists... maybe not right away, but you get the idea. This model of specialization has led us to our current social environment.

Tribal existence itself was driven by survival modality. The group was only going to survive, in most cases, if they worked together. Their numbers provided valuable security. The tribe needed to protect themselves from nature, wild animals, other tribes or aliens (since we're guessing). It is likely that this mode carried over into the early stages of specialization under the flag of survival. In essence, technological advances benefited the tribe, making "group influence" the first currency. As time passed and groups became too large to keep a local mental impression cognitive, they would offshoot into subcultures and soon become their own new tribe. Eventually this value of tribal group influence was replaced by military force influence through advanced technologies in weapons and armor, coupled with larger and larger groups.

Off balances in technology, due to regional natural resources, likely led to some of the earlier empires. Areas with greater natural abundance of the grains and grasses that could be stored for future consumption were also areas that spawned the earliest and most powerful empires, according to Dr. Diamond. It makes sense that regions that had this advantage plus other natural resource advantages, like copper and tin, had greater advances in their technology. This led to cities, militaries and empires, which outgrew other less fortunate regions. Empires could dictate, through force, how entire regions would live under their rule. Force influence became a mode for accumulating more and more wealth and citizenry, by controlling vast regions and people.

The Roman Empire epitomized this in their rule over places like Egypt and its wealth of grains. This great empire was led by its military strength. Even the leadership of Rome was, at times, subject to the ruling military force. At one point this control was threatened by Cleopatra's influence over two of Romes greatest leaders, Julius Caesar and Mark Anthony, but the militarist's force influence was ultimately left in power under Augustus. For thousands of years this mode of influence ruled the great populations of the West until a man named Nathan Rothschild changed all that. Nathan Rothschild, son of Amsel Rothschild, a check writer (banker), successfully reorganized the entire mode of influence in the early 1800's and never fired a shot.

Michael Light

Chapter 13 - The Rothschild Shift

Nathan Rothschild started his investment career in England exporting textiles. He later expanded into metals, securities and trading currencies. In the meantime his father Amschel had secured an opportunity to invest some of the fortune of King William the Hess, of the Netherlands, which he sent to Nathan. Nathan, along with his four brothers, had organized a network of agents around Europe that delivered gold and information, which eventually led to a coup d'etat of the entire British economy. His couriers were often the first back to England with news that would have an effect on the London markets.

When Napoleon was about to invade the Netherlands, Hess gave Amschel Rothschild the task of removing his rather substantial fortune out of harm's way – out of the hands of Napoleon's invading forces. Amschel was left holding the largest fortune in Europe, which found its way to Nathan in England. This fortune combined with Nathan's extensive spy networks to create one of the greatest effects in the history of influence.

From 1811 on, the Rothschild network of agents were responsible for the delivery of gold to pay Wellington's troops in their war against France. In the defining battle of the war, the Battle of Waterloo, Nathan's agents were able to deliver to him the news that England had won the battle. Nathan had received this news a full 24 hours before the government messengers had arrived. It was well known that the Rothschilds had an extensive spy network, and the morning after Nathan received the news he proceeded to the markets and sold off his holdings of English currency. This news swept through the markets and left everyone else with the impression that France had won the battle, which would hurt the British currency.

Everyone began selling off the British notes and when the dust had settled and the price had bottomed out, Nathan bought every bit of it for pence on the pound. When the news finally arrived in London that England had won the battle the pound quadrupled in value, and the Rothschild family owned all of it. He followed with a similar move on the French Franc and in just a few days, through his brilliant bluff in the markets, became the most influential man alive. He could now dictate these two governments' policies through his control of their economic fates. "Currency influence" was now king!

Michael Light

Chapter 14 - Socialmedia Influence

As of today, riots have been raging in England for two days. This morning on Bloomberg News online there was an article about looters using Blackberrys to organize looting. According to the article, authorities asked Blackberry to shut down their chat services until order could be restored. In the same article Blackberry was quoted as "doing their part," pointing out that these same services were being used to organize clean-ups and protection as well. Some people might find Blackberry's response appalling, but Blackberry is right for several reasons. The most obvious being the Murdoch rule.

Bay Area Rapid Transit, in San Francisco, once shut down cell phone services in their commuter stations to avoid a "possible protest," and people in the Bay Area completely freaked out. I'm not sure what rights British citizens have, but in America, the right to freedom of speech is the foundation and basic principle of our Constitution. These types of actions and requests by those in authority really point out the nervousness they have about this freedom. More specifically they fear the tools that allow people to communicate with each other, for good or less than noble reasons. I seems like a lingering Freud thing.

There really isn't a question about whether or not this kind of communication should be stopped, or allowed, but rather that it doesn't seem that it can be controlled. Even if every company chose to side with the authorities in every case, the fact remains that there are twenty other brilliant code writers out there waiting in line to be the next MySpace. And people adjust quickly. If Blackberry chose to shut down their chat, it would only hurt

Blackberry, because it is pretty unlikely that whatever authority was responsible for the request is going to pay their bills or recoup the losses in their market share.

When I consider this information coupled with what they are now calling the "Middle East Spring," I can't help but side with the idea that there are larger powers at work – call it evolution or whatever – it's all happening. It may be out of any individual powers' control, be that government control, economy-based or even groups of individual online users. The entire World, from Mozambique to Nova Scotia, is plugged in, and everyone is watching everything that's trending. It is an amorphous volume of voices and the one thing that gives anyone of us more say than anyone else is your Socialmedia Influence. Klout's API is being used to gauge the value of someone's perk-worthiness. Companies are checking it when we reserve a hotel room, and this is just the tip of the iceberg. Some day, socialmedia influence may be the only currency accepted. One of my friends mentioned a restaurant that only accepts donations. There are no prices on the menu, and the idea has been so successful that they are opening a second location. People with no money can have rice and dal and no one is turned away. How's that for a business plan. Their CPA must be bald.

The fact is that the entire money supply of the World is what they call a fiat currency. It is not based on metals, grains or anything, but the faith people have in its value. In essence, people can decide on whatever they want to call currency. And if one fails, It is likely humanity will create or decide on another. This has been the case throughout history. Currencies have come and gone. They have been based on everything we can imagine from beads to paper notes.

It's origin is based in the compression of goods or services in one form or another, and it is whatever we decide it is as a group. But what happens when we change the basic paradigm and choose to allow another to decide, for themselves, the value of our services, like the restaurant I mentioned. It could actually turn out to be a much better motivation for the quality of those services. Or what if we choose to set up regional trade relations, through group sites, while locally offering each other the basic human needs as a grant to living, without asking for anything in return? Could the Internet become the tool for it? It could very well be similar to the effects of the donation only restaurant.

All things considered, money has become a force of influence that guides the entire momentum of events and policies around the World. It is no longer just a form of compressed time and space. It has in fact become a decision we offer as a way to face the challenges all human beings on some level suffer. And now we're beginning to see the subtle glimpses of a shift in human perception that has its roots throughout history.

I think we are seeing a change that will affect everything we know, very soon. It's happening now. If you think about it, very few people would do most of the things they do, everyday, if they weren't being paid for it. My question, which I consider to be Buckminster Fuller's original thought, is; "What would people do if all their time was free?" My guess is that they would do magnificent things with extraordinary motivation! It's what made Western Civilization a force in the first place. It was originally called specialization, and it was born from accumulating wealth in the form of grain surpluses.

Michael Light

Summary

Communication has been at the heart of every shift in human existence, and whether that communication was through language or technology, it is evident in every process along the way. This current stage of communication is by far the most advanced we've ever seen, and the crazy part is that it is advancing faster and faster every day. Soon we will be able to fold up our 65 inch flex panel and pack it for our vacation to wherever, so we can see and hear the entire World live and breathe each new moment. I am one of those people who spends way more time out in nature, normally, but have found myself glued to this shift. My window has been my gadgets and I know that the news will fly any minute now! "Everything Just Changed!"

The thing that gives me a sense of peace is something I have spent my whole life watching and listening for... the message that every thing is Okay! The Internet has shown me that people are way more empathetic to each other than they are selfish. I mostly see it with their close friends, but that circle is growing more and more online, through the various socialmedia sites we use to develop our personal communities. I see it when I see my friends post about the causes they are close to, or when there is a disaster that affects their lives. They reach out and people come together to help. It's a part of our nature that lingers from the time when our ancestors were in the same tribe, that together we can face anything!

For the last 20 years, I have been listening to the crowd chant "2012" and "Armageddon" with a belief that something bad was coming to end our days. I sometimes wonder if they had the same fear of the unknown just before the Renaissance in Europe. It shifted our whole perception to hear things like the

Earth is NOT flat, and that there are laws that govern motion and the elements of nature. It must have been terrifying for some people. Hell, they were killing people who claimed to think outside the box, and using religion to justify it.

So here we are again, ready to evolve into something new, and all that mainstream society can see is the unknown about it. I had a conversation with someone a few hours ago. We were talking about retirement. He suddenly throws out this whole shit storm theory about the end and how technology was going down with one electromagnetic pulse. I thought to argue the logic of that idea, as there is no such device, but it wasn't worth wasting my time. People want to believe in doom, sometimes more than they are willing to change anything about their lifestyles, regardless of how destructive or wasteful those lifestyles might be! I can see how this would play out in the mind as totally devastating!

I see something entirely different happening right now. I see a global community being defined by the motivations of our natural state as empathetic beings. We are sharing our World with each other, instead of trying to take it from each other. I see it testing every paradigm of capitalism and consumerism, and I see it without a leader. It is an amorphous inertial response to thousands of years of ideas that have sought to control the "irrational exuberance" of humanity's "mob mentality," and is revealing the idea as false. We don't need a global police force when we have each other as a community!